j574.5
JP66c

COASTS and SHORES

Rose Pipes

RSVP

RAINTREE
STECK-VAUGHN
PUBLISHERS
A Steck-Vaughn Company

Austin, Texas

Published by Raintree Steck-Vaughn Publishers,
an imprint of Steck-Vaughn Company

A ZOË BOOK

Editors: Kath Davies, Pam Wells
Design & Production: Sterling Associates
Map: Sterling Associates
Illustrations: Cecilia Fitzsimons

Library of Congress Cataloging-in-Publication Data

Pipes, Rose.
 Coasts and shores / Rose Pipes.
  p. cm. — (World Habitats)
 "A Zoë Book" — T.p. verso.
 Includes glossary and index.
 Summary: Introduces some notable coasts and shores around the world, including the Great Barrier Reef, the Orinoco delta, and the sandy coasts of the British Isles.
  ISBN 0-8172-5008-5
  1. Coasts — Juvenile literature. [1. Coasts.] I. Title. II. Series: Pipes, Rose. World habitats.
 GB451.2.P66 1999
 577.5'1—dc21   97-46755
                                                 CIP   AC

Printed in Hong Kong by Midas Printing Ltd.
Bound in the United States
1 2 3 4 5 6 7 8 9 LB 02 01 00 99 98

Photographic acknowledgments

The publishers wish to acknowledge, with thanks, the following photographic sources:

Martin Barlow - title page; / Environmental Images / Vanessa Miles 28; / Impact Photos / Xavier Desmier-Cedri - cover inset tr, 25; / John Cole 17; NHPA / Ralph & Daphne Keller 10; / Melvin Grey 15; / T.Kitchin & V.Hurst 16; / Kevin Schafer 22; / David Woodfall 27, 29; South American Pictures / Tony Morrison 20, 21; Still Pictures / Kelvin Aitken - cover inset bl; / Edward Parker 9; / Yves Lefevre 11, 13, 19; / Anne Piantanida 23; / Thierry Thomas 24; TRIP / B. Turner 8; / J. Stanley 14; / Ask Images 18; Woodfall Wild Images / Ted Mead - cover background, 6; / David Woodfall 7, 26; / George Gornacz 12.

The publishers have made every effort to trace the copyright holders, but if they have inadvertently overlooked any, they will be pleased to make the necessary arrangement at the first opportunity.

Contents

All the words that appear in **bold** are explained in the Glossary on page 30.

Different Types of Coasts

The place where the land meets the ocean is called the coast. Coasts may be sandy or rocky, and they can be flat or steep. Some coasts are a mixture of all these things.

Waves create many of the shapes at the

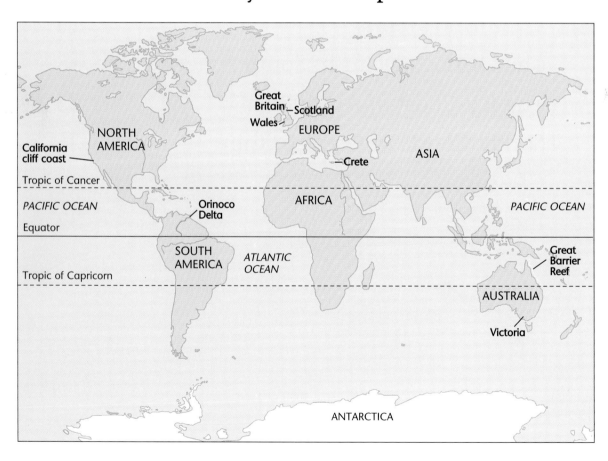

On this map you can see the names of coasts and shores that you will read about in this book.

coast. They cut cliffs in the land and make caves and arches in the rocks. Waves can wear away parts of the rocks over many years.

Wind also shapes the coast. It blows sand from beaches to form hills and ridges of sand, called **dunes**. Dunes are somewhat protected from **erosion** by plants and grasses. Both wind and water can cause erosion.

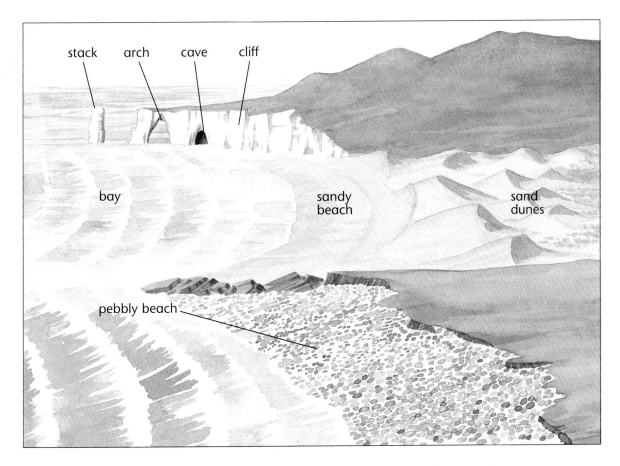

In this picture you can see different types of coasts.

Wildlife on Coasts

There are many different coastal **habitats**.
These are affected by climate and rainfall.
Each has its own kinds of plants and wildlife.

Here is the coast of Victoria, in southern Australia.
Flowering plants grow on top of the steep cliffs,
but few plants grow on the shore or on the rocks.

Shore birds live on sandy and muddy seashores. They hunt for small animals, such as sand crabs, that live on or in the sand and mud.

Seals, sea otters, and other animals and birds live partly on land and partly at sea. Puffins catch fish from the sea. In June and July, they come to the land. They make burrows there or in cracks in the rocks where they lay their eggs.

The gannets in this picture live on Bass Rock, an island off the coast of Scotland. They dive for fish in the sea and make nests on the rocky island.

Life and Work on Coasts

On many coasts people make a living by catching and selling fish. They also work in coastal towns called vacation **resorts**.

This photograph shows fishing boats on the coast of Crete.

Visitors come to these towns for vacations.

Waste material from towns and factories is pumped into the ocean or sea. It **pollutes**, or poisons, the ocean water, and kills animal and plant life. Some coasts are polluted too, and swimming is dangerous.

Oil from ships may spill into the ocean and onto coasts. The oil kills seabirds and other creatures that depend on sealife for food. There have been many major oil tanker spills.

In 1996, an oil tanker hit rocks and spilled its oil into the ocean near this oil terminal at Milford Haven in south Wales.

The Great Barrier Reef, Australia

A reef is a ridge of rocks below the sea. The Great Barrier Reef is made of **coral**. It is the

This photograph was taken from an airplane flying above part of the Great Barrier Reef.

longest coral reef on Earth and lies off the east coast of Australia. It is really a series of reefs that stretches for about 1,250 miles (2,010 km).

The coral skeletons build up to form the reef. The reef is growing all the time. Parts of it stick up above the warm, shallow water.

Corals are tiny sea animals. There are more than 350 kinds of corals in the reef. Some corals have hard skeletons. Others, like the ones in this picture, are soft and grow in feathery fan shapes.

Many different life forms dwell in the reef. Most of the fish are brightly colored. They have good eyesight, and the colors help them to tell each other apart.

This anemone fish lives among the tentacles of the sea anemone. The fish is safe here, because the anemone is poisonous to most other sea animals.

The reef was once in danger from oil drilling. But, in 1975, Australia made it into a marine park to **protect** it.

Another danger is the crown of thorns starfish. It eats the living coral and has destroyed parts of the reef.

Thousands of people visit the reef. They travel in glass-bottomed boats, or swim and dive to see the corals and other life there.

California's Cliffs

In California, between the cities of Monterey and San Luis Obispo, there is a very beautiful

The waves here are often very big,
and they crash against the steep cliffs.

cliff coast next to the Pacific Ocean.

There are no towns on this steep coast, only a few houses, hotels, and restaurants. No one lives on the shore. But people visit this area to see the wildlife and the breath-taking scenery here.

Many birds nest on the cliffs. These peregrine falcons are **birds of prey**. They eat ducks, terns, and other birds and can dive 124 miles (200 km) per hour.

Seals and sea otters swim along or rest on the shore. The otters nearly died out because they were hunted for their fur. Now sea otters are protected, and about 2,000 live here.

Sea otters eat shellfish. They hit the shells with stones to break them open.

A two-lane road runs above the cliffs along the coast. Bridges form the arch to carry the road over **canyons** in the cliffs.

The road is sometimes dangerous. It is often foggy, and in winter there are wild storms. The rain washes rocks and soil onto the road.

In the winter of 1982, there were more than 40 **landslides**. The road was blocked for many months.

This picture of the Big Sur coastline shows a bridge over one of the canyons.

The Orinoco Delta in South America

The Orinoco River flows into the ocean on the coast of Venezuela. Near the coast, it splits into many channels with islands in

The Orinoco Delta is almost the size of Maryland.

between. This is called the Orinoco Delta. Palm trees grow on much of the delta, and mangrove trees grow near the ocean.

Some large wild animals live in the delta channels. There are crocodiles and a **mammal** called the manatee.

Manatees live in the water. They eat plants that grow in the water and on the banks.

This manatee is swimming under the water. Manatees are protected in some areas, but they are still in danger of dying out. Humans are the only enemies of the manatee.

The Warao people live on the delta.
Warao means "canoe people." They make

The Warao people build houses on stilts, like this one, to keep them above the floodwater. They make the stilts from tree trunks, and they thatch the roof with palm leaves.

canoes out of palm wood and use them for fishing and traveling around the delta.

Cattle farmers also live on the delta. When the land floods in the wet season, they move their cattle by boat to higher ground where it is dry.

In this picture, a Warao woman is making small baskets out of palm leaves. People also weave these to make hammocks and mats.

The Icy Coast of Antarctica

Antarctica is a **continent** that is covered with ice. It is hard to see where the coast is, because ice also covers the ocean for most of the year.

These emperor penguins are standing on an ice shelf off the coast of Antarctica.

Only a small part of an iceberg sticks up above the water. If a ship hits an iceberg, the ship may be damaged and sink. Sometimes, **tugs** are used to tow the icebergs away from the paths of ships.

When thick ice reaches the ocean, huge lumps may break off. When they break, the sound echoes like a gunshot on the water. These lumps are called icebergs.

These huge chunks of ice float into the ocean. Look at the boat in this photo. Now imagine the size of these icebergs.

In winter, the ocean around Antarctica freezes. Ships cannot sail through the ice. Scientists who live in Antarctica must wait

This helicopter is bringing supplies to scientists living in Antarctica.

until summer for supplies to arrive by ship. These scientists study the winter sea ice and the animal life on this cold continent. They also hope to learn how changes here affect the world's climate.

The ocean around Antarctica is home to many animals, such as whales, seals, penguins, and fish. Each animal has **adapted** to this harsh climate.

The Weddell seals shown here have their young on land in the summer. In winter, they live under the ice in the ocean.

Sandy Coasts of Great Britain

Some of Great Britain's sandy coasts are in wild places where few people live. Others are close to cities and towns.

Sandwood Bay is on the northwest coast of Scotland. No roads lead to the bay, which is many miles from the nearest village or town.

Few plants grow on Britain's sandy beaches, but thousands of animals live there. Many of them have shells, and some burrow down into the sand.

Birds such as oystercatchers and curlews have long beaks. They poke their beaks into the sand to find worms, mussels, crabs, and other food to eat.

Some birds, such as terns, nest on pebbly beaches or in dunes. Nesting in large groups means there will be enough food for the young. Also, the young terns have a better chance of being protected and of surviving.

An oystercatcher digs for worms in the sand.

In winter, it is too cold to swim or sunbathe. The beaches are empty except for the birds that visit from colder, Arctic lands.

In summer, thousands of people visit many of Britain's sandy beaches. This beach in Dawlish, Devon, is always crowded on hot, sunny days.

Some of Britain's beaches win awards each year. The awards tell people which beaches are the cleanest and safest.

Other beaches are still dirty and unsafe. They may be polluted by oil spills from ships, called tankers, on the oceans or seas. Tourists leave litter on the beaches. This makes the beaches dirty and in some cases unhealthy.

This blue flag shows that the beach has won an award.

Glossary

adapted: If a plant or an animal can find everything it needs to live in a place, we say it has adapted to that place. The animals can find food and shelter, and the plants have enough food in the soil and enough water. Some animals have changed their shape or color over a long time, so that they can catch food or hide easily. Some plants in dry areas can store water in their stems or roots.

birds of prey: Birds that hunt other animals for food.

canyons: Deep narrow valleys. There is often a river at the bottom of a canyon.

continent: One of the seven large landmasses in the world. They are Europe, Asia, North America, South America, Australia, Antarctica, and Africa.

coral: A small sea creature. Some corals have hard skeletons, or casings, that form a kind of rock, also called coral.

dunes: Hills of sand made by the wind. They are found in deserts and next to the sea.

erosion: The wearing down of earth or rocks by the action of water, wind, or ice.

habitat: The natural home of a plant or animal. Examples of habitats are deserts, forests, and coasts.

landslide: The sliding of rocks, soil, or stones down a slope.

mammals: The group of animals whose young feed on their mother's milk.

polluted: Dirty or poisoned. Polluted water contains waste materials. The waste may be poisonous or dangerous to humans or wildlife.

protect: Keep safe from changes that would damage the habitat.

resorts: Villages or towns that people visit for vacations.

tugs: Small ships that are used to pull, or tow, larger ships or other heavy things.

Index